DISCOVERING THE GOSPEL OF MARK

Sixteen
Studies

by
Jane
Hollingsworth

InterVarsity Press
Downers Grove, Illinois 60515

Sixth printing, February 1975

© 1943, revised edition © 1966
by Inter-Varsity Christian
Fellowship of the
United States of America.

InterVarsity Press is the book
publishing division of Inter-Varsity
Christian Fellowship, a student
movement active on campus at
hundreds of universities, colleges
and schools of nursing. For more
information about Inter-Varsity
Christian Fellowship, write IVCF,
233 Langdon, Madison WI 53703.

ISBN 0-87784-419-4

Printed in the United States of America

contents

ACKNOWLEDGMENT

The author wishes to acknowledge a debt of gratitude to The Biblical Seminary for the method of study followed in this booklet. Particularly is she grateful for the concrete help received from Dr. Caroline L. Palmer under whom she studied the Gospel of Mark.

Introduction

This booklet has been prepared for individuals who have expressed a serious desire to study the Bible, and will not be useful to those who do not share this determination. These studies are not Bible outlines, but directions for study in the Gospel of Mark, and may be used either in groups or individually. Each group participant may benefit by having a copy of this study guide, because each study has questions for individual preparation for the next group study.

This particular approach to the book of Mark has several specific aims. It is not the only approach—or necessarily the best, and certainly not the easiest; but personal use and the evaluation of others indicates that this method has merit. It will open up the Scriptures in a new way to those who will faithfully pursue it.

The AIMS of this study are to help you: (1) *grasp the facts* of the Gospel as written by Mark, just as they appear on the page, (2) *develop a skill* for studying the Bible independently (If you burrow in and make a real business of this study, you will emerge with a better idea of how to understand the Word of God without a human teacher and without "devotional helps."), (3) *develop a more robust spiritual life* by watching the majestic figure of the Son of God as He walks through the pages of Mark with divine authority and redeeming love. In thus watching, may you obey the will of God as revealed through Him.

directive procedures

General procedure is outlined in each study, but you will need to refer to this introductory material for specific directions. Beginners in this study method usually find it slow, sometimes mechanical, and often painful, but always rewarding. There is additional satisfaction and joy in reaching a goal which has taken time and effort.

Because of the paragraph divisions and more up-to-date language, you will find the REVISED STANDARD VERSION of the Bible a helpful aid to this study.

use a notebook

Writing keeps your mind from wandering and prevents you from ineffective skimming. Keeping a separate notebook for every book in the Bible will enable you to form a private commentary of study notes. If possible use loose-leaf so that insertions can be made at the proper places. Make out the form of the notebook at the beginning so that you do not waste time writing notes on odd pieces of paper.

Make your notebook simple or complicated, according to your taste. The minimum suggested is sixteen blank pages for the chapter studies. Also, provide a page for each of the following studies:

1. TRAINING OF THE TWELVE DISCIPLES—in the first chapter Jesus says, "Follow me and I will make you become . . ." As you study, notice *how* He makes the disciples what he wants them to be.

2

2. OPPOSITION—note that Jesus' works, words, travel, and death are closely connected with this subject.

3. JESUS' CONSCIOUSNESS CONCERNING HIMSELF AND HIS MISSION—the question "Who then is this?" is raised in the first chapter. Since so many people refuse to believe that Jesus is the Son of God, we should search diligently to determine what He thought of Himself.

4. WHO—is this Jesus? This question is on the chart. (See following procedure for *Use a Chart.*) Note each situation out of which this question arises and how the understanding of His followers progresses. The turning point in the book comes over this issue and it is of climactic importance.

Many other subjects such as, Prayer, Faith, and Evangelism would also make valuable studies. In addition to the subject studies, pages could be designated for questions concerning critical problems, data concerning authorship, notes taken on messages from and about the book, characteristics of the book as a whole, a map, and an index.

read Psalm 119

A part of Psalm 119, the Bible study Psalm, is suggested as spiritual preparation for each private study or discussion group. The Psalm is full of prayers for direction and understanding for studying the Bible. Spend only two or three minutes reading it.

listen to the Holy Spirit

I once heard of an art student who visited an art gallery in New York City to study one picture. He spent hours in front of it and acquired what he considered a fairly accurate idea of its meaning. As he turned to leave, a man touched him on the shoulder and asked if he would like to know what the artist had in mind when he first painted it. The student responded politely, and the stranger began to unfold the background, history, and purpose of the picture with such depth of feeling that the student was thrilled with an appreciation which his hours of study had not produced. Who was the stranger? The artist, of course. How much the student would have missed if he had been in too big a hurry to listen to the stranger! Since the Master Artist unveils the mysteries of eternity, the Bible student overlooks much if he studies without help.

The Holy Spirit, who alone knows the things of God (I Corinthians 2:10-11), is waiting to teach you. Listen to Him and obey as He speaks. Begin each study time with prayer for His illuminating ministry.

observe the facts

Accurately observe what Mark has written. Do not go into its meaning, nor apply it to your life. Do not search critically—nor read passively. But *do* approach the chapter with the unspoiled attitude of the three-year-old and *do* what he would with a new object: *inspect with ardent curiosity, fervent imagination,* and *experimental inquiry.*

Test your ability at this type of inspection by observing the facts in the first Psalm. Read to see what is there.

> Blessed is the man
> who walks not in the counsel of the wicked,
> nor stands in the way of sinners,
>   nor sits in the seat of scoffers;
> but his delight is in the law of the Lord,
>   and on his law he meditates day and night.
>
> He is like a tree
>   planted by streams of water,
> that yields its fruit in its season,
>   and its leaf does not wither.
> In all that he does, he prospers.

4

The wicked are not so,
> but are like chaff which the wind drives away.
Therefore the wicked will not stand
> in the judgment,
> nor sinners in the congregation of the righteous;
for the Lord knows the way of the righteous,
> but the way of the wicked will perish.

What objects do you find? Do you discover that the Christian is stable like a tree instead of easily blown about like the chaff? If so, you are not observing; you are interpreting.

Do you observe a tree? a seat? ways and a Way? water, green leaves, wind? a congregation? These are the observations. Only *after* you have made the observations concerning the facts are you ready to explain the meaning. Remember to write the observations in your notebook.

use a chart

Each paragraph is given a name (for complete explanation see Study 1, question 3). This paragraph name or title is to be written on the chart in the back of this booklet. At first you may consider the chart a waste of time and inferior to outlining. But the chart is used for three reasons: (1) you gain a *view of the whole book;* (2) for the chart you *compress thoughts into one or two words* (The thought which is expressed in one word is more easily understood than the one which is expressed in a sentence.); (3) you have a *clue to memory.* Your words on the chart are of little value in themselves; they are useful only as they suggest to you the contents of the book.

directions for individual study

1. *Live* with the book of Mark throughout your study. Reading some of Mark in your daily devotions will make it mean more to you.

Since much of Mark was originally spoken before an audience, *reading aloud* will help you relive the circumstances. Study the situation and attempt to reproduce it.

2. *Review* often. Keep the main thoughts of the book in mind by using the chart.

3. *Observe* the facts.

4. Discipline yourself to record thoughts, observations, and answers in your notebook. If the devotional thought brought out by the study questions does not meet *your specific need,* consider the other ideas in the passage. Constantly ask "How does this affect my life?"

5. *Cultivate the art of meditation.* One basis for this is memorized verses. When riding on a bus or train, instead of letting your mind wander, recall some portion of Mark and relate its meaning to present situations.

6. *Discuss* what you are learning with your friends. If possible use thoughts and illustrations from Mark in your next talk or lecture.

7. *Memorize.* Learn each verse in its context so that

when you quote the reference you can relate the circumstances under which it was spoken. (Memorized verses are of inestimable value in personal work.)

If you have trouble memorizing, try this procedure: first, get the meaning; then, separate the parts. Repeat the verse or section from memory several times until you can say it easily without much thought. Recall it from memory —without looking—in half an hour, in twenty-four hours, and again next week. If you do, you will have it for life.

8. *Pray* into your life everything you learn from Mark.

9. *Prepare* for the Bible study group by (a) reading the assigned chapter, (b) observing the facts, (c) naming the paragraphs (See Study 1.).

directions for a group leader

The success of the group study mainly depends on your preparation. Prepare the entire chapter before the study. (If possible follow the directions for individual study.) Leading does not mean delivering the facts in the form of a lecture. It means that, as a question is studied, you will know enough about it to recognize the answer when it is discovered by the group, summarize the findings—and pass on to the next question.

It is much more difficult to lead a discussion than to make a talk, but with these studies the process should be simplified. Each participant should have a Bible open in front of him so that each one can find answers, and the results can be pooled.

1. *Open* the study by (a) reading a section of Psalm 119, and (b) praying for the guidance of the Holy Spirit.

2. *Review* only briefly. Much time should be given to individual review, but the group should spend only a short time reviewing the previous chapter. Next, have any study reports. (See following direction 6.d.)

3. *Ask* for the fact observations. If several have not read the material, have everyone watch for facts while someone quickly reads the chapter.

4. *Call* on someone to give paragraph titles. Think through the events of the chapter using the words as cues.

8

This type of summary is an excellent way to grasp an overview of the contents. (See Study 1, question 3.)

5. *Work out* the text and application questions together. As the leader, summarize whenever necessary. If available, a blackboard is helpful. Encourage the others to put group discoveries and conclusions in their notebooks.

6. It is your responsibility to *direct the discussion* and to acknowledge the person who wants to contribute something.

    a. *Restrain* the person who is aggressive, has a dominant personality and/or tends to do all the talking by directing questions to the more reticent ones, who often have much to add.

    b. *Keep* the group from discussing tangents. Tangential discussion often grows out of the study, but in order to cover the main points of the Bible passage such digressions should be left for another time.

    c. In handling the discussion, *limit* the amount of time spent on any one question. When the points have been discovered, go on to something else.

    d. When questionable points, doubts, or criticisms come up, *ask* the person most interested to look it up and make a report at the next study. The report should not exceed three minutes.

7. *Close* the study with (a) five to ten minutes of general comments (suggestions, comparison of notes, or devotional thoughts) and a quick summary and (b) prayer. Suggestions for prayer are given with each study.

8. Encourage individual preparation for the next study.

Note the verbs used in these directions for group leadership. Then compare with verbs in the directions for individual study.

Mark 1

read, pray

1. Set the tone of the study by reading Psalm 119:1-8. Pattern your opening prayer from the desires and petitions of the Psalmist. (You can learn to pray by studying the ones who pray and their prayers in the Bible.) Ask the Holy Spirit for definite guidance.

observe

2. Read the first chapter of Mark as though you had never seen it before. In this first reading you are not trying to get depth of meaning, the proper interpretation, or a new spiritual truth to apply to your life. You merely want to *observe* the outstanding facts — not the details, but the features which strike your attention.

Ask yourself these questions and discover how much you have observed (do this hastily):

    a. WHO? Who were the people present?

    b. WHAT? What is said about them? What happened?

    c. WHERE? What country, city, house, location, scene is mentioned?

    d. WHEN? Is the day, time of day, or any passing of time mentioned?

    e. STYLE. What do you notice about the author's style and vocabulary? Does he use action, description, little or much detail, repeat words?

3. The first chapter has ten paragraphs. See the chart for divisions. In order to keep the succession of ideas clearly in mind, give to each paragraph a name of not more than three words. Find a word or phrase which is unique to the paragraph and will best recall it to your mind. For instance, you might use "John the Baptist" for the first paragraph.

Insert these names on the chart. You may have many names suggested; select the best one for the study group. For individual charts, each person should use the name that recalls the material for him.

4. Answer the following questions about Jesus. Use your notebook to jot down ideas of particular value.

a. What are His various works?

b. Over what forces did He display power?

c. Is there a problem in your life to which this same Jesus can apply His power?

d. What emotions did He experience? Why?

e. What do you find to substantiate the statement that He is the Son of God?

f. What shows that He was also truly human?

g. In verse 27 the people in the synagogue were amazed at His *authority*. The scribes and Pharisees quoted traditions as their authorities. What is your impression of Him from this passage?

5. Study the people.

a. Before Jesus helped someone He had to make a contact with that person. How were these contacts made?

b. What does this suggest as to how contacts may be made between the Lord Jesus Christ and people in your university?

c. Every time Jesus demonstrated His power, the witnesses responded in various ways. Note these responses.

(1) How do you respond to demonstrations of Jesus' power?

(2) Compare your responses with those recorded in this passage.

6. For the study, TRAINING OF THE TWELVE DISCIPLES, quickly jot down the first step in that process which is found here. In what way does this apply to you?

summarize, pray

7. Summarize the main points. Close with prayer, asking that the ideas you learned in this study will become part of your daily living.

prepare

8. Prepare for the next study:

a. Read Mark 2-3:6. One reading takes three minutes.

b. Observe the facts: WHO? WHAT? WHERE? WHEN?

c. Name the paragraphs and write each name in proper order on your chart.

Mark 2

read, pray
1. Read the second division of Psalm 119, verses 9-16. Incorporate thoughts and words from the Psalm into your opening prayer.

review
2. Review the previous study in two or three minutes. Use the paragraph titles on your chart to recall and organize that chapter. Next, have any prepared reports.

observe
3. Discuss your observations on the facts.
a. WHO?
b. WHAT?
c. WHERE?
d. WHEN?

4. What is the author's style? Quickly consider:
a. Are his sentences short and to the point or long and involved?
b. Does he use figures of speech?
c. Does he draw contrasts or comparisons?
d. Does he use questions and direct discourse?

name paragraphs
5. Choose a name for each paragraph and write it on the group chart.

Find the relationship between paragraphs. Express the connection in one word and place it on the curved line on the chart. For example, in paragraph two Levi was called, and in the next they feasted at his home; thus, "Levi" is a connecting word.

answer

6. In the first paragraph, verses 1-12, the Son of Man demonstrated His authority to forgive sin.

   a. How did this event affect
      (1) the scribes?
      (2) the paralytic?
      (3) the spectators?

   b. Why did Jesus forgive the paralytic before he healed him?

   c. All of those present heard Jesus' words of forgiveness, but how many were actually forgiven?

   d. Is this supreme work of the Savior always done on an individual basis?

   e. Have you ever known the healing forgiveness of "My Son, your sins are forgiven"?

7. In verses 15-22, what is Jesus telling the people seated at His table?

   a. Why did He use the four similies?

   b. What does each one mean?

8. What is the purpose of a "sabbath" day?

9. For the OPPOSITION study answer the following:

   a. What people, in the first paragraph, opposed Jesus?

   b. Who were the opposers in the other paragraphs?

   c. This whole chapter hinges on opposition. There is a step of progression in each of the first three paragraphs and a climax in the first paragraph of chapter three. Find these steps:

    (1) What aroused the people's opposition each time?

    (2) How was it expressed?

    (3) Note their increased boldness.

10. For the study on JESUS' CONSCIOUSNESS CONCERNING HIMSELF AND HIS MISSION, find and jot down three statements in this chapter which reveal His consciousness of His mission.

summarize, pray

11. Summarize briefly. Have a short period of silence for individual meditation and close with several sentence prayers (oral).

prepare

12. Prepare for the next study:

a. Read Mark 3:7-35.

b. Record a few observations: who, from where, what?

c. Find the meaning of each paragraph and place the descriptive name on your chart.

d. Meditate on: (1) ways you can make your association with Jesus more meaningful (vv. 13-19), (2) the reply Jesus gave His mother and brothers (vv. 31-32).

e. Memorize verse 35.

Mark 3

1. Read the third division of Psalm 119, verses 17-24. Pray for "open eyes" as you study.

2. Quickly go over the chart for review. Using your paragraph titles as clues, think through chapters one and two. Do you have a special report for this study?

3. Pool your preparatory observations: who? from where? what?

4. Choose paragraph titles for the group chart. Indicate paragraph connections on your chart.

5. A crowd follows Jesus.

a. Why did so many people follow Jesus in paragraph two? Who were they?

b. Who did Jesus order to keep His identity secret? Why?

6. For the study, TRAINING OF THE TWELVE DISCIPLES, write three reasons why the twelve were appointed and

organized (vv. 13-19). Then reduce each reason to one word.

a. Are these three things still necessary in training for Christian service?

b. Discuss ways you can make your personal association with Jesus more meaningful.

7. What did Jesus' friends think of Him in verses 20-21? Put this in your own words by imagining yourself as one of His friends in that mob.

a. What guests from Jerusalem were present on this occasion?

b. Why is it significant that they were from Jerusalem?

c. How did Christ answer the guests' explanation of His power?

d. Why was it a good answer?

e. Study the way Jesus answered questions to help you talk with others.

8. Study the unforgivable sin. Especially consider it in the light of the situation in which it was spoken.

9. Explain the attitude of Jesus' family in verses 31-32.

a. *Imagine* yourself sitting in the crowd that had gathered about Jesus. How would you respond when you heard His words, "Behold, my mother and my brothers"?

b. Are you satisfied that you are meeting the condition for this spiritual kinship?

summarize, pray

10. Reiterate the main points. Have silent prayer; then have two or three close in prayer.

prepare

11. Prepare for the next study:

a. Read Mark 4.

b. Observe: who? what? when? where? What striking features do you see?

c. Name each paragraph. Write the names on your chart.

d. Do the parables naturally follow the previous chapter? Explain why or why not.

Mark 4

read, pray

1. Read the fourth part of Psalm 119, verses 25-32. Find an appropriate prayer.

review

2. Review briefly and have study reports.

observe, choose titles

3. Pool your findings from individual study.

a. Observations: who? what? when? where? Did you find any striking features?

b. Name each paragraph and write the name on the chart.

c. Do these parables naturally follow the previous chapter? Why or why not?

answer

4. In the parable of the Sower (the Soils), give your description of each type of character depicted in the type of soil.

a. Can you classify yourself as one of these?

b. What are the great enemies of the receptive character?

c. Name some specific circumstances or situations that make it hard to be receptive in your university or community.

d. If you were to bear fruit a hundredfold, what specific

changes would you have to make? List in your notebook.

5. Why, do you think, do two of the five verses about the parable of the lamp admonish men to listen and to heed what is said?

6. In verses 26-29, what message of encouragement is given to the man who casts seed upon the earth? Who is he?

7. How appropriate at this time in Christ's ministry was the simile of the mustard seed which is less than all seeds?

8. Consider Jesus as a teacher:
a. What makes Him interesting?
b. How does He stimulate thought?
c. Are any of His students more advanced than others?
   (1) Upon what basis?
   (2) Where are you?
d. Do you think He would have used the same stories if His rostrum had been a soap box in New York City instead of a little boat pushed off the shore of the Sea of Galilee? Why or why not?

9. Read the last miracle in this chapter, verses 35-41. Absorb every move, sound, word, and emotion. Imagine. Listen. See. If you had been on that boat, how would you describe to a friend what happened?

This storm was not usual. The sturdy fishermen lived on the lake. They knew every mood of its fickle winds. After a day of listening to Jesus, they had taken the lead in bringing "him with them, just as he was, in the boat" (note vv. 34-36), and now they were in despair.

a. Do you think their teacher was expecting too much faith? Why or why not?
b. Can you expect the Lord to make a "storm" a laboratory to see how well you have understood?

c. In verse 41, the disciples asked the most significant question of Mark's book. They had just witnessed Christ, *the Ruler of all nature,* speak to the howling wind and swelling waves.

(1) What is this question?

(2) How would you answer it?

summarize, pray

10. Briefly summarize the main points of the study. Then, worship Jesus in silent prayer. Thank Him for His power. Have one person close with oral prayer.

prepare

11. Prepare for the next study:

a. Read Mark 4:35 through chapter 5.

b. Who went where? How did they get there? What were the main events?

c. How many times do you notice the boat in this chapter? Where have you noticed it before?

d. Write each paragraph name on your chart.

Mark 4:35-5

read, pray

1. Read Psalm 119:33-40. Think about the requests made to God here and make your own requests.

review

2. Using the chart, review chapters 1 to 4:
a. What had been the growth of opposition?
b. How did the disciples come in?
c. What had been the picture of Christ so far?
d. Was anyone sure of His identity?

If there are any special reports have them now.

observe

3. Briefly discuss the observations (two minutes):
a. What were the events?
b. Who was there?
c. Where were they?
d. How did they get there?
e. How many times is the boat mentioned?

name paragraphs

4. Select a title for each paragraph and place on group chart.

answer

5. Compare the four miracles. Make four parallel col-

umns in your notebook and briefly answer all the questions on each miracle.

a. Force   *storm, legion, woman, daughter*

b. Need   ____ ____ ____ ____

c. Response   ____ ____ ____ ____

____ ____ ____ ____

d. Faith   ____ ____ ____ ____

e. Recovery   ____ ____ ____ ____

f. Results   ____ ____ ____ ____

____ ____ ____ ____

g. Christ   ____ ____ ____ ____

h. You   ____ ____ ____ ____

a. Over what *force* did Jesus display His power?
b. To what extreme had the *need* gone?
c. How did those concerned *respond* toward Jesus before and after?
d. What was the place of *faith?*
e. What was the extent of *recovery?* Give the remark which indicates this.
f. What were the *results?* How far-reaching were they?
g. What is the picture of the person of *Christ?*
h. Is this same power exercised in *your* life?

6. See how well you observed the facts in the story of Legion by answering the following questions in a few words.

a. Where did the man live? Why didn't someone tame him?

b. In what two ways did he express himself?

c. What two contradictory attitudes did he show toward Jesus?

d. Did Jesus address the man and the demons as one or separately?

e. Under what circumstances did Jesus give this man instructions for the future?

f. When did Christ leave? What influenced His decision to depart?

7. As Jesus was on His way to heal Jairus' daughter, the woman with the plague touched Him.

a. Why did He stop and expose the woman when she had already been healed?

b. What additional blessing came to her through the conversation?

c. How did this blessing differ from the former one?

8. Notice that Jesus told the man formerly possessed by Legion to go home and tell his friends, but He told the people who witnessed the raising of Jairus' daughter that no man should know it.

a. Why did Jesus urge a testimony in one place and forbid it in another? (Consider the difference in location. Consider also that the serious opposition of the Jews had taken place in the same general vicinity in which Jairus lived.)

b. Are we as Christians supposed to testify on any and every occasion? How do you know when you should testify?

summarize, pray

9. Refer to the comparison of the four miracles for your brief summary. Close with a time of prayer in which you ask the Lord to make His power real in your lives.

prepare

    10. Prepare for the next study:

a. Read chapter 6.

b. Observe the people involved in the incidents.

c. Compress the thoughts of each paragraph and write an appropriate name for each on your chart.

Mark 6

read, pray

1. Read Psalm 119:49-56. Pray for direction to live out what you learn.

review

2. Review chapter 5 and have any special reports.

observe

3. In observing, particularly note the people and where they were.

name paragraphs

4. Give names for the paragraphs; write them on the chart.

answer

5. In paragraph one, what questions did the people from Jesus' home town (Nazareth) ask Him?

   a. How did they respond to His teaching, works, and claims?

   b. How did their response affect His work?

6. Twice in this chapter the question of Jesus' identity comes up—once in the first paragraph and again in the paragraph on Herod. Both times a personal reason was involved. The first reason may be summed up in the word *familiarity;* the second in the word *conscience.* (Sometime

in your personal study trace Herod's dealings with John the Baptist to see how Herod came to have such a guilty conscience.) Note these two facts on the page designated WHO.

a. Consider the question of familiarity which arose at Nazareth. How did familiarity with Jesus prove a barrier?

b. Discuss for a few minutes how you could hinder a work of the Lord by thinking you know Him better than you do.

7. Make a comparative chart for the two feasts in this chapter:

	Herod's feast	*The 5,000*
Guests	*lords, high captains, chief men*	*those who sought Jesus*
Time		
Entertainment or Activity		
Motive		
Place held		
Power exercised		
Result		
Surplus food?		

8. For the study on TRAINING OF THE TWELVE DISCIPLES answer the following questions.

a. Where, why, and how did the disciples go (vv. 7-13)?

b. What did Christ give them?

c. What was His negative charge?

d. What positive charge did He give them?

e. Were they to take much equipment and make extensive preparation?

f. What were they to expect from the people to whom they ministered?

g. How do you know they were to be satisfied with the hospitality they received?

h. What was their message?

i. What were the results (vv. 12-14)?

j. What followed their work (v. 30)?

k. After they had made their reports, what were they invited to do?

l. Why didn't they rest?

m. What did they learn that made the interruption worth-while?

n. What do you learn from this incident about your own time of meditation and rest with the Lord?

o. What did they learn about Jesus from the sea incident (vv. 45-52)?

summarize, pray

9. Discuss any questions and summarize briefly. Close with two or three sentence prayers.

prepare

10. Prepare for the next study:

a. Read chapter 7.

b. Observe.

c. Turn to the map in the back of your Bible and quickly trace the trip Jesus made in this chapter. Begin with His arrival in 6:53. The other places are recorded in 7:24 and 7:31.

From the time Jesus went into Tyre and Sidon until He started His final journey to Jerusalem, He remained either in Gentile country or in the lonely regions of northern Galilee.

(1) What attitude of the religious leaders led Jesus into Gentile country?

(2) Note briefly what occurred in each location.

d. Name the paragraphs and insert the names on your chart.

Mark 7

read, pray

1. Read Psalm 119:41-48. Notice especially verse 42. In the seventh chapter of Mark, Jesus brilliantly answered those who reproached Him. Pray that you will understand the "word of truth" in your study.

review

2. Quickly review by using the chart. Take time now for special reports.

observe

3. Share observations of facts.

name paragraphs

4. Go through the chapter briefly giving each paragraph a name for your chart.

answer

5. Start at the beginning of the chapter and find the answers as you read. Some of these answers will apply to the study on OPPOSITION.

   a. What is tradition? (This is not in the text.)

   b. What was the tradition mentioned here?

   c. Who brought up the question? Why?

   d. What three groups of people did Jesus address (vv. 5, 14, 17)?

e. What did He say to each? Why?*

f. What was wrong with the tradition of the Pharisees?

g. In the light of the explanation which Jesus made to the disciples in verses 18-23, what, do you think, would He say concerning the following opinions?

(1) Filth defiles a man's soul. A man born in the slums and reared in poverty can hardly be blamed for low spiritual ebb.

(2) I'm religious enough. In fact, I do everything the church requires. I've been confirmed and baptized. I go to church every Sunday, and take communion. I can't see that God should hold anything against me.

6. When the Syrophoenician woman came to Jesus, He was in Gentile territory and had evidently retired there with the hope of being alone with His disciples.

a. Find a statement which shows He had not come to minister to the multitudes, but wanted privacy.

b. Why did Jesus not respond immediately to the woman's request?

c. Consider the answer the woman received from Jesus. Was this remark applicable only to this woman, or might He have made it to any Gentile?

d. What do you learn about Christ from this incident?

e. What lesson in prayer can you as a Christian learn from this woman?

*Corban: According to an accepted tradition, a person could pronounce the word *corban,* which means gift, over any property; then the property was regarded as dedicated to God. The tradition also stated that, even though this property could not be given to any other person, it could be used by its owner for his gratification and delight. Thus, it was possible for a man to let his parents live in poverty while he lived in great wealth.

7. In the paragraph on the healing of the deaf-mute, consider:

a. What request was made of Jesus?

b. Who made it?

c. The method of healing: why did the Lord use this method with this particular man?

d. What did Jesus do for the man when He looked up into heaven?

e. Compare the way Jesus responded to the people's request in verse 32 with the way they responded to His request in verse 36.

f. What inconsistency of life do you find in verses 36 and 37?

summarize, pray

8. Summarize by giving Jesus' responses to the different needs brought to Him. If there are any truths in this chapter which you feel should become a part of your life, pray silently about them. Close by singing a prayer hymn.

prepare

9. Prepare for the next study:

a. Read chapter 8 through 9:1.

b. Observe the facts.

c. Name the paragraphs and place on your chart.

Mark 8 - 9:1

read, pray

1. Read Psalm 119:57-64. Open with an appropriate prayer.

review

2. Have a brief review and any study reports.

observe, choose titles

3. Observe the facts.
a. Share outstanding impressions about this chapter.
b. Place approved titles on the chart.

answer

4. Compare this feeding of the 4,000 with the one of 5,000 in chapter 6.
a. How long had they been without food?
b. What part did the disciples have?
c. How much food was left over?
d. What is the chief spiritual lesson?

5. Find an impertinent insult in this chapter.
a. Why was it an insult?
b. Why did Jesus not comply with the request?

6. To what kind of bread was Jesus referring in verses 14-21? To what kind were the disciples referring?

7. Leaven was an accepted symbol of evil and corruption.

a. Think about the teaching of the Pharisees. Can you put in one word what the leaven of the Pharisees was?

b. What was the leaven of Herod? Think about the account of Herod's feast which resulted in the murder of John the Baptist.

(1) What type of life was that?

(2) Why would Jesus warn the disciples against it?

8. What caused Jesus to make the blind man see?

a. Where did it take place?

b. What method was used?

c. Why did He use a physical means?

d. Can you think of any reason this should have been only a partial healing?

9. On the way to Caesarea Philippi what important question did Jesus ask about Himself?

a. What did the disciples answer? (Compare the lack of spiritual understanding in verse 21.)

b. Why is this called the main crisis in the book so far?

c. How do *you* answer this all-important question?

10. After Peter identified Jesus, what did He begin to teach the disciples?

a. Verses 34-38 are called *The Great Renunciation*. To whom were they spoken?

b. If you practiced this 100%, what changes would you have to make?

11. TRAINING OF THE TWELVE DISCIPLES:

a. In verses 14-21 find two things learned.

b. In verses 27-30 find one thing concerning Jesus' person.

c. In verses 31-38 find four things concerning their relation to Him.

summarize, pray

12. Allow five minutes for discussion and summary. Close by praying for the courage to follow Jesus.

prepare

13. Prepare for the next study:

a. Memorize and meditate on verses 34-38. Be able to recite them by the next study, giving the circumstances under which the words were spoken.

b. Go through the review of the first eight chapters of Mark.

c. Read Mark 9:2-50.

d. Observe.

e. Name the paragraphs. Write the names on your chart.

review A

You have completed the first section of Mark in chapter eight. You should spend time individually in definite review. Perhaps you could take one review question a day during your private Bible study time. By so doing you would not have to give more than five minutes at a time, and the review would prove of more value. The more often you recall what you learn, the sooner it becomes your own.

1. Give the main divisions of the book.

2. Over what forces did the Lord Jesus Christ exercise His power in this book? Give an example of each and tell what chapter it is in.

3. Go through the book, paragraph by paragraph, using the names on your chart as clues. Recall the substance of each paragraph—from memory if possible.

4. What have you found in Mark to make you think Jesus Christ is human?

5. What from the first chapters of Mark leads you to think Jesus is divine? What is He that other men are not?

6. Think through the experiences of the disciples as they were being trained by Jesus. Concentrate on the main points in the call of each, the commission, etc.

7. To what about Jesus did the scribes and Pharisees object?

Mark 9

1. Read Psalm 119:65-72. Pray for "good judgment and knowledge."

review

2. Depending on your particular group, review briefly chapters 1-8 or only chapter 8.

a. Have someone recite Mark 8:34-38 and give the circumstances under which it was spoken.

b. Does someone have a special report?

observe, choose titles

3. Quickly pool observations and paragraph titles.

answer

4. Study the five major events from Mark 8:27 to 9:29.

a. Give one central idea in each incident.

b. Why this particular sequence of events?

5. Consider the transfiguration.

a. What supernatural things took place?

b. Why did Peter make his suggestion?

c. What did the transfiguration mean to the disciples concerning:

(1) The Person of Christ?

(2) His future death?

(3) Future glory (8:38)?

(4) The Pharisees' accusation that He broke the law of Moses?

6. Answer the following questions about the healing of the demoniac.
a. Of what did the people accuse the disciples?
b. Whom did Christ rebuke? Why?
c. What question did the disciples ask in verse 28?
(1) Why is this a healthy attitude for a Christian?
(2) Are there any questions which you should ask the Lord about yourself?
d. What did Jesus answer?
e. Can you see any connection between the failure of the disciples and the attitude of the father?
f. What responsibility does this place on the Christian?

7. Why were the disciples afraid to ask Jesus what He meant by His teaching in verse 31?

8. What illustration did Jesus use to teach the disciples humility?

9. Compare verses 38-41 with the disciples' question in verse 28. To what kind of service does "a cup of cold water" refer?

10. Add to the disciples progress for the study on TRAINING OF THE TWELVE DISCIPLES.

11. Explain verses 42-49. What connection did this teaching have with *The Great Renunciation?*
a. What does this mean to you?
b. Is there anything you have been doing, any place you have been going, anything you have been seeing that could cause you or anyone to stumble?
12. Salt without seasoning (taste) is insipid and worthless.

a. What are the various ways in which salt is used?

b. What things gave seasoning to the life of Jesus as you have seen Him in Mark?

c. What things are salt and seasoning to the Christian's life?

summarize, pray

13. Summarize and allow time for questions. Close with two or three praying briefly.

prepare

14. Prepare for the next study:

a. Read and observe from chapter 10.

b. Name paragraphs and place the name and relations between the paragraphs on your chart.

c. Memorize verse 45.

Mark 10

read, pray

1. Psalm 119:73-80. Choose thoughts appropriate to Bible study for your opening prayer.

review

2. Take a few minutes for review and reports.

observe, choose titles

3. Observe. Place paragraph titles on the chart. Share the main impressions received from your reading.

answer

4. The Pharisees and Sadducees had differing opinions about divorce. They came to Jesus to see which side He would take.

   a. What did Jesus answer them?

   b. How did He explain Moses' treatment of divorce?

   c. What did Jesus give as the basis for His answer?

   d. In verse 11 Jesus was explaining verse 9. To whom did He speak?

   e. Today we hear much about love being the chief virtue of the marriage relationship. Judging from the answer given here to the disciples, what, do you think, would Jesus consider the chief virtue?

5. What principle did Jesus teach in the paragraph about children?

6. Study Jesus' conversation with the rich young ruler.

a. What was the young man seeking?

b. What was Jesus leading the young man to admit in verse 18?

c. How did the man usually respond to the commandments of God (vv. 19-20)?

d. What was Jesus' attitude toward him?

e. Why did the Son of God give this particular answer to the man?

f. Why did he go away sorrowful?

g. Why did the young man forfeit the thing for which he came?

h. Would giving up his possessions bring eternal life? What would?

i. Consider your own possessions. They may be something other than riches. Would the Lord have to ask you to give them up before you could follow Him?

7. Why did Jesus' teaching on riches amaze the disciples? Relate verses 29-31 to His teaching on riches.

8. Jesus forecasts coming events.

a. Where were they going in verse 32?

b. Why were they amazed and afraid?

c. Compare the three announcements of Jesus' death— 8:31, 9:31, 10:32-34.

d. What further teaching does He give in the third?

9. The question of status was as prevalent then as it is now.

a. What caused the tense situation among the twelve in verses 35-45?

b. Were the ten more noble than the two? Why?

c. Contrast the hierarchy of men with the way of God in verses 42-45.

d. What was revealed for the first time in 10:45 about

Jesus' mission in the world? Add this answer to your study page on this subject.

10. In verses 46-52 what was the outstanding quality of the beggar's faith?
   a. What did Jesus do to make his faith more concrete?
   b. Compare *your* faith with his.

11. In this chapter four young men and a blind man faced life: Jesus, the ruler, James and John, and Bartimaeus.
   a. What did each ask of life?
   b. What was each prepared to give?
   c. What are *you* asking?
   d. What are *you* willing to give?

summarize, pray
12. Quickly summarize. Quote together verse 45 as a closing prayer.

prepare
13. Prepare for the next study:
   a. Read Mark 11:1-26.
   b. Observe: who? what? where? when?
   c. Place names of the paragraphs on your chart.
   d. Memorize 11:24.

Mark 11:1-26

read, pray

1. Read Psalm 119:81-88. Notice that a reason is given for every petition. Use this method in your opening prayer.

review

2. Have someone review chapter 10 by using paragraph titles. Have the special reports prepared since the last study.

observe, choose titles

3. Share your factual observations. Place on the chart names of the paragraphs in Mark 11:1-26.

answer

4. In connection with Jesus' activities:

a. Note the number of times He went in and out of Jerusalem.

b. Note the references to time of day and passing of time. Is this particularly characteristic of Mark?

c. What important week in the life of Jesus begins in this chapter?

d. Where did Jesus reside during His stay in Jerusalem?

5. Jesus assumes several different roles.

a. Locate and explain His function as:

   (1) physician

   (2) king

   (3) prophet

(4) supreme authority

(5) teacher

(6) judge

b. Is His ability equally effective in each role? Why?

c. Contrast with your own versatile abilities.

6. Consider Jesus' pre-crucifixion days:

a. Since Jesus knew He was going to be crucified, how do you explain the triumphal entry?

b. What shows that the entry was not impromptu on Jesus' part?

c. What did this entry mean to the people (vv. 9-11)?

d. What did this incident mean to the disciples? Recall how they had expected the Messiah to come.

7. Carefully study the fig tree incident.

a. In verses 12-14, why did Jesus expect to find fruit on the fig tree?*

b. What was said that leads you to believe the fig tree was situated in an advantageous position?

c. What people with whom Jesus dealt appeared, like the fig tree, to have fruit because of outward signs, but did not?

8. Jesus' actions carry out His words.

a. Who did Jesus throw out of the temple? Why?

b. Why did no one resist Him as He purged the temple?

c. Describe Jesus on this occasion.

9. Jesus and the disciples again pass the fig tree.

a. How did Jesus answer Peter's comment about the fig tree?

b. In this paragraph the Teacher used three words:

*The Palestine variety of fig bears an immature crop of green fruit called "taksh." Absence of this fruit indicates that no mature figs will follow.

whoever, whatever, whenever. What are the three main ideas which follow these introductory words?

c. What experience would be necessary in a person's life for him to pray with the kind of faith mentioned in verse 23?

summarize, pray

10. Summarize briefly. Test verse 24 in closing sentence prayers. Invite everyone to join.

prepare

11. Prepare for the next study:

a. Memorize verse 24—if you didn't do so before the study.

b. Read Mark 11:27 through chapter 12.

c. Observe.

d. Name paragraphs and write the names on your chart.

Mark 11:27 - 12

read, pray

1. Read Psalm 119:89-96. Open with prayer.

review

2. Have different ones recite 8:34-38, 10:45, and 11:24. Briefly review the main incidents since they started on the journey to Jerusalem in 10:32. Has someone prepared a special report?

observe, choose titles

3. Quickly go over the observations. Select names for the group chart.

answer

4. From 11:27 to 12:37 four major questions were brought to the Messiah. The paragraphs are built around these questions. See chart. Answer the following questions about each question brought to Jesus:

    a. What occasion brought up the question?

    b. What was the motive?

    c. What answer was expected?

    d. What answer was given?

    e. What was the result?

    f. What underlying truths were presented?

    g. What was new to the twelve in this teaching? (Note this under TRAINING OF THE TWELVE DISCIPLES.)

5. Jesus instigates a climax to the questioning.

a. What question did Jesus bring up when He mentioned David?

b. How was this a climax to the questioning?

6. What are the three reasons Jesus said "beware" of the scribes (vv. 38-40).

7. What was the contrast between the scribes and the widow in the next paragraph?

8. Share ideas from this study that you want to incorporate into your daily living.

summarize, pray

9. Summarize; then consider verse 24 in your closing prayer.

prepare

10. Prepare for the next study:

a. Read Mark 13.

b. Observe: when, where, and under what circumstances was this discourse given?

c. Write paragraph names on your chart.

Mark 13

read, pray

1. Read Psalm 119:97-104. Pray for understanding.

review

2. Review and have reports.

observe

3. Observe: when, where, and under what circumstances was this discourse given?

name paragraphs

4. Name the paragraphs. Write the names on the group chart.

answer

5. What distinct, concrete events are mentioned as coming in the future? In answering consider the following about the catastrophes:

a. Which are national? Which ones refer to the Destruction of Jerusalem in A.D. 70?

b. Which are international?

c. Which are political?

d. Which are social?

e. Which are social and economic?

f. Which are religious?

g. Which are in the realm of nature?

6. What specific experiences are to be the disciples'?
a. What task did they have that made it necessary for them to take heed (vv. 9-10)?
b. Why should they not be anxious?
c. Why should they remain faithful?

7. What warnings were given?

8. What were false signs? true signs?

9. List the things which shall accompany the coming of the Son of Man.

10. What did Jesus tell them they could not know?

11. Note the progress in the TRAINING OF THE TWELVE DISCIPLES.

12. What was revealed that was new about JESUS' CONSCIOUSNESS CONCERNING HIMSELF AND HIS MISSION?

13. Apply verses 37-38 to yourself and your group.
a. What does it mean to watch?
b. How could you be more watchful?

summarize, pray
14. Have a brief summary. Close by praying that you will not be deceived. Ask several to participate with sentence prayers.

prepare
15. Prepare for the next study:
a. Read chapter 14.
b. Observe and relive the situations from the viewpoint of Peter.
c. Name the paragraphs.

Mark 14

read, pray

1. Read Psalm 119:105-112. Does your testimony agree with that of the Psalmist? Open with prayer.

review

2. Review the events of the week from the triumphal entry. What progress was the opposition making? Are there any reports?

observe, choose titles

3. Discuss observations. Select and write paragraph names on the group chart.

answer

4. Mary anoints Jesus.

a. Relate the paragraph of Mary's anointing with the one before and the one following.

b. What motive justified Mary's extravagance?

c. When does charity take a secondary place?

d. Estimate the value that the Lord Jesus put on human service.

5. This section is full of contrasts. See how many you can find. Note especially these:

a. Great love—great hatred.

b. Words of unparalleled praise—words of unparalleled doom.

c. Great faithfulness to a cause—great faithlessness.

6. Note JESUS' CONSCIOUSNESS CONCERNING HIMSELF AND HIS MISSION.

a. How was His foreknowledge of time and events emphasized by the fact that the Pharisees determined otherwise? Compare 14:2 with 14:28-30.

b. What did He reveal concerning the purpose of His death in verses 23-24?

7. Look at Judas' plot in verses 10-11. With this in mind, can you think of any reason why, in the next paragraph, Jesus sent the disciples to meet a "man bearing a pitcher"? Why did He not just give them the name and address?

8. Jesus gives the New Covenant.

a. Around what does the New Covenant center (vv. 22-25)?

b. What, do you think, did this mean ot the disciples?

c. What does it mean to us?

d. Look at the two preceding paragraphs. In what two ways was preparation made for the New Covenant?

9. What new things were added to the TRAINING OF THE TWELVE DISCIPLES in this chapter?

10. Trace Peter's experience.

a. What traits of character does he show each time he is mentioned? Note how each incident was a step which logically followed the one before.

b. In the last paragraph, verses 66-72, what were his specific answers in the denial?

11. Study Jesus during this crucial time in His life.

a. List the things which show the voluntariness of His death.

b. List the things which show the tragic loneliness of His death.

summarize, pray

12. Allow a few minutes for general discussion and questions; then summarize briefly. Share prayers of thanksgiving and praise for the work and glory of God through Jesus Christ.

prepare

13. Prepare for the next study:

a. Read chapter 15 as though you were an assigned newspaper reporter.

b. Jot down your observations.

c. Name the paragraphs. Using your chart, include the paragraphs of both chapters 14 and 15 under these headings: Preparation, New Covenant, Struggle and Arrest, Trials, Crucifixion, Burial.

Mark 15

read, pray

1. Read Psalm 119:113-120. Pray for clear understanding.

review

2. Review and have reports.

observe

3. Observe the facts.

name paragraphs

4. Choose names for the paragraphs and write them on the group chart.

answer

5. Compare the ecclesiastical trial in 14:53-65 with the civil trial in 15:1-20.

a. Who was the judge in each?

b. Who were the jury in each?

c. At what hour was each held?

d. What was the charge in each?

e. What was the mockery in each?

f. What was the difference in the attitude of the high priest and Pilate?

g. What part did the chief priests have in the Roman trial?

h. Describe Pilate as he appeared in this trial.

i. Who was really condemned at this trial?

j. Note the silences of Jesus.

k. Describe Jesus as He appeared in these trials.

6. Give six incidents in which Jesus suffered at the hands of many.

7. Locate the references to prophecy.

a. What prophetic words were spoken?

b. What prophecies were cited as being fulfilled?

8. Three groups deride and revile Christ while He hangs on the cross.

a. Who were they?

b. What did they say? Why?

c. In what way was the accusation in verse 31 true?

d. Why could Christ not answer the challenge of His enemies and come down from the Cross? Compare 10:45.

e. Why did Jesus not even give a spoken reply to the revilers?

f. In what ways do you answer when reviled? Why?

9. Find at least four unnatural and unusual things in the paragraph from verses 33-41.

10. What do the following contribute to the meaning of the death of the Son of God:

a. Verse 34—the forsaken cry,

b. Verse 38—the rending of the veil,

c. Verses 37-39—the mode of death?

11. The religious leaders, the rulers, the multitude, and even the seemingly indifferent Roman soldiers were forced in the face of this—*the greatest climax in human history*—to answer the question WHO? In your opinion, who answers right and who answers wrong?

summarize, pray

12. Have someone briefly summarize chapters fourteen and fifteen. Allow time for each person to have private prayer. Close with sentence prayers; invite everyone in the group to participate.

prepare

13. Prepare for the next study:

a. What is your answer? Who is this One who claims to be the Messiah, the King, the Son of God, the Savior of the world?

b. Meditate on what you have learned about Jesus Christ: how He came into the world, suffered the horrors of loneliness, desertion (even by God the Father), persecution, and death so that He could pay the ransom for *your* sin.

c. Jesus healed and changed the lives of those who believed He could and would. His power is just as effective now as it was during His earthly life. Have you ever told Him that you believe and, in response, had His power operating in your life?

d. Read chapter 16.

e. Observe: who? what they did? where they went? what they saw? how they responded?

f. What, if anything, is unusual about the literary structure?

g. Name the paragraphs and write names on your chart.

h. Think about the influence of this chapter's events on the past twenty centuries.

Mark 16

read, pray

1. Read Psalm 119:121-128. Thank the Lord for accounts of Jesus' life which give you understanding.

special reports

2. Leave your review for the end of this study, but, if there are any, have the prepared reports now.

observe

3. Observe: who? what they did? where they went? what they saw? how they responded?

name paragraphs

4. Write paragraph names on the chart.

answer

5. WHO is Jesus?

a. How are verses 1-8 a climax to this question?

b. What do verses 9-20 add?

6. Study the resurrection.

a. Did the disciples steal Jesus' body? Explain why or why not.

b. What evidence do you find for the bodily resurrection of Christ?

c. In verses 9-20, how many and what appearances are given?

d. What do they add to the story? Why are they recorded?

7. How do these events rebuke Jesus' OPPOSITION?

8. What is new concerning the Person and work of Jesus in this chapter?

9. How are verses 14-19 a climax in the TRAINING OF THE TWELVE DISCIPLES?
a. Why did Jesus reprimand the disciples?
b. What made it possible for Jesus to give instructions and then leave?
c. What is the responsibility of one who knows Jesus is risen?

10. Discuss personal responses.
a. Is there a command for you to obey?
b. What promise(s) can you claim?
c. What error should you avoid?
d. Is there power for you to use?

review
11. Summarize the last three chapters.

pray
12. Invite everyone to participate in conversational prayer.

The review study which follows may be used for individual study or another group study.

review B

1. List the main divisions of the book.

2. Recall the key verse, giving the reference. How can you divide the book by this verse?

3. Name two situations in which Jesus showed His superiority to demons. Where are these found?

4. Give the references and tell the stories of two people whom Jesus healed.

5. What are two instances in which Jesus indicated the necessity of faith?

6. Think through and write down the progress and climax of the opposition to Jesus.

7. Outline the training that prepared the twelve disciples.

8. Concerning Jesus:
a. How does Mark show the importance of *who* Christ is?
b. What was Jesus' most important work?
c. List five things you discovered about Jesus in Mark.

9. What would you say to a friend who asked you to explain why you call Jesus your Savior?

10. Review often what you have learned. Relate it to the immediate context and the overview of Mark, and you will have it for life.

do it again

You have just completed a method of intensive, analytical Bible research. This same method can be used for other books of the Bible. You don't need a study manual! Develop your own as you study.

1. Use the directions in the INTRODUCTION of this booklet.

  a. Remember to ask for the help of the Holy Spirit.

  b. Live with the Bible book you are studying.

    (1) Meditate on it.

    (2) Talk about it.

    (3) Memorize verses in context.

    (4) Review often.

2. View the whole before you begin to dissect the parts. If you see the whole first, the parts will have more meaning. Whenever possible begin your study *by reading the entire book at one sitting.*

3. Always look for information. *Read to get an impression or to find specific facts.* For instance, if you were reading Philippians you might notice that the word "fellowship" is repeated throughout the letter. Write the following things about fellowship wherever it is found.

  a. WHO has it?

  b. WHAT kind of fellowship is it?

  c. WHY do they have it?

  d. WHEN did they have it?

  e. WHERE were they?

  f. AFTER gathering *all* the data, make some conclusions.

4. Study the characters mentioned. Learn all you can about them. Imagine them as people you would meet and talk with on your city's main street. Invite them home for lunch.

5. Ask yourself, *What* is said and *Why* it is said. Everything in the Bible is in a particular place for certain reasons. Can you discover them?

6. Observe connections. You may find a conjunction which indicates that the words and ideas which follow have a definite logical connection with the words and ideas which have preceded. These conjunctions are the words, *and, but, wherefore, therefore,* etc.

7. Geography is important. Ask yourself, *Where* did it happen? Such discovery will not only make the incident live for you, but it may clarify an obscure meaning.

8. Historical background is interesting and enlightening. The customs, habits of life, and events from secular history which parallel biblical ones often add invaluable information to the subject.

9. Look for the spiritual lessons which the people in the Bible learned or which God wanted them to learn. Apply them to your life. Ask yourself:
   a. What is the main point?
   b. Does it apply to me, and have I learned it?
   c. Is there a promise I can claim?
   d. Is there a command I should obey?
   e. Is there an error I should avoid?
   f. What is new for me to learn about my God and **Savior?**

study chart

CHAPTER / VERSE			
1	1-8	*John the Baptist*	Christ's PREPARA-TION *for His ministry*
	9-11	*baptism*	
	12-13	*temptation*	
	14-15	*Gospel of God*	Christ's PROCLAMA-TION *of Himself*
	16-20		
	21-28		
	29-31		
	32-34		
	35-39		
	40-45		
2	1-12		
	13-14	*Levi called*	*Levi*
	15-17	*feasting*	
	18-22		
	23-28		
3	1-6		
	7-12		

"The Son of man came not to be ministered unto, but to minister . . . . Who Is He? . . .

3 13-19 _____

20-30 _____

31-35 _____

4 1-9 _____

10-20 _____

21-29 _____

30-32 _____

33-34 _____

35-41 _____

5 1-20 _____

21-24 _____

25-34 _____

35-43 _____

6 1-6 _____

7-13 _____

14-29 _____

30-44 _____

45-52 _____

53-56 _____

7 1-23 _____

24-30 _____

31-37 _____

9 1

2-8

9-13

14-29

30-32

33-37

38-50

10 1

2-12

13-16

17-22

23-31

32-34

35-45

46-52

11 1-10

11

Christ's
PASSION
and death

... but to minister

... and to give His life a ransom for many." . . . . Mark 10:45

11 12-14 _____

15-18 _____

19 _____

20-26 _____

27-33 _____

12 1-12 _____

13-17 _____

18-27 _____

28-34 _____

35-37 _____

38-40 _____

41-44 _____

13 1-2 _____

3-8 _____

9-13 _____

14-23 _____

24-27 _____

28-32 _____

33-37 _____

14 1-2 _____

3-9 _____

10-11 _____

14 12-16 _____

17-21 _____

22-25 _____

26 _____

27-31 _____

32-42 _____

43-50 _____

51-52 _____

53-65 _____

66-72 _____

15 1-5 _____

6-15 _____

16-20 _____

21 _____

22-32 _____

33-41 _____

42-47 _____

16 1-8 _____

9-11 _____

12-13 _____

14-18 _____

19-21 _____

and to Give his life a ransom for many." . . . . .MARK 10:45 (key verse)

for further study from InterVarsity Press

LEADING BIBLE DISCUSSIONS
James Nyquist compiles practical, field-tested suggestions to help leaders prepare, lead and evaluate Bible studies. paper, $1.25

DISCUSSIONS ON THE LIFE OF JESUS CHRIST
These twelve Bible studies consider the basic message of Christianity—the character of Christ, the implications of his claims. paper, $1.25

LOOK AT LIFE WITH THE APOSTLE PETER
Jane Hollingsworth and Alice Reid help individuals and groups uncover spiritual treasures from Peter's life and writing. paper, $1.25

GROW YOUR CHRISTIAN LIFE
This guide directs personal Bible study on topics such as personal evangelism, sin and growth, knowing God's will and Christian marriage. It can be used by both individuals and groups. paper, $1.95

LEADER'S NOTES TO GROW YOUR CHRISTIAN LIFE
Peter Northrup gives at least three possible outlines for leading a weekly discussion group on each of the twelve topics covered in *Grow Your Christian Life*. paper, 95¢